INTER

OF ACTIVE AND

PASSIVE VOICE

PATTERNS AND

EXAMPLES

MANIK JOSHI

<u>Dedication</u>

THIS BOOK IS

DEDICATED

TO THOSE

WHO REALIZE

THE POWER OF ENGLISH

AND WANT TO

LEARN IT

SINCERELY

Copyright Notice

****

IMPORTANT NOTE

This Book is Part of a Series
SERIES Name: "English Daily Use"
[A Thirty-Book Series]
BOOK Number: 12
BOOK Title: "Interchange of Active and Passive Voice"
****

Table of Contents

Active and Passive Voice

VOICE - Definition

Voice refers to the form of a verb that shows whether the subject of a sentence performs the action or is affected by it. Or

Voice refers to the position of the action verb in a sentence relative to the subject and the object. Or

Voice refers to the relationship between the doer (the one who performs the action) and the action (verb).

ACTIVE VOICE - Definition

The form of a verb in which subject is the person or thing that performs the action.

In an active voice sentence, the subject acts on the object.

The active voice emphasizes the actor (the doer of the action).

Active voice is the direct writing, which means the subject does the verb's action.

Example:

They finished the work.

[subject -- "they", verb -- "finished", object -- "work"]

In this sentence, the subject (they) acts on the object (work).

Other Examples:

The *teacher* **praises** him.

She **posted** the letter.

I **buy** new books.

We **will celebrate** his birthday.

They **proposed** changes to the social system.

PASSIVE VOICE - Definition

The form of a verb in which subject is affected by the action of the verb.

In other words, the form of a verb in which subject of the sentence has an action done to it by someone or something else.

In passive voice the subject is acted upon.

The passive voice emphasizes the receiver of the action.

Passive voice is the indirect writing style, which means the subject receives the verb's action.

Important Note -- The object of the active voice becomes the subject in the passive voice.

Example:

The *work* **was finished** by them.

[subject -- "work", passive verb -- "was finished", object -- "them"]

In this example, the subject (**work**) is not the doer; it is being acted upon by the doer '**them**')

Other Examples:

He *is praised* by the teacher.

The **letter** *was posted* by her

New **books** *are bought* by me.

His **birthday** *will be celebrated* by us.

Changes *have been proposed* to the social system by them.

WHEN TO USE PASSIVE VOICE

It is generally advised to use the passive voice sparingly because use of the active voice makes your writing direct, clearer, concise, explicit, more natural and vibrant. A sentence in active voice flows more smoothly. It is easier to understand than the same sentence in passive voice. However, using passive voice is preferred in the following situations:

(1). You should use passive voice when *you do not know the active subject*. *Passive* -- Syllabus of the school **has been changed**. (We don't know who changed it.)

(2). You should use passive voice when *active subject is not important and you want to make the active object more important*. *Passive* -- Passengers **were alerted**. (It is not important to know who alerted them.)

(3). You should use passive voice when *active subject is obvious*. *Passive* -- Three persons **have been arrested** for committing a theft. (obviously by the police)

(4). You should use passive voice when *you want to emphasize the action of the sentence rather than the doer of the action*. *Passive* -- *More than hundred people* **were killed** *in plane crash.*

(5). The passive is frequently used *to describe **scientific or mechanical processes** to avoid the personal pronoun or to emphasize the research and not the researcher*. *Passive* -- The experiments on animals **are being conducted** regularly.

(6). *The passive is often used in **news reports**: Passive* -- *Your concerns* **have been conveyed** *to the administration.*

(7). *Sometimes, the sentence in the active voice does not sound good. And we use only the passive voice when speaking or writing:*

Active -- His mother **bore him** in Japan in 1985. [sounds awkward]
Passive -- He **was born** in Japan in 1985. [sounds good]

Active -- We call him Doctor Brown. [sounds awkward]
Passive -- He is called Doctor Brown. [sounds good]

(8). You can use passive voice when you want *to make more polite or formal statements.*

Active -- You have not completed the project. [less polite]
Passive -- The project **has not been completed**. [more polite]

(9). You can use passive voice *to avoid responsibility.*
Active -- We made a mistake.
Passive -- A mistake **was made**.

(10). You can also use passive voice *for sentence variety in your writing.*
(11). You can also use passive voice when you want *to avoid extra-long subjects.*

NOTE:
Avoid shifting from active to passive voice or passive to active voice in the same sentence because it can cause awkwardness and confusion.

CORRECT: I **played** football, and my friend **watched** movie. (consistency of active voices)
CORRECT: Football **was played** by me, and movie **was watched** by my friend. (consistency of passive voices)

INCORRECT: I **played** football, and movie **was watched** by my friend.
(shifting of voices from active to passive)
INCORRECT: Football **was played** by me, and my friend **watched** movie.
(shifting of voices from passive to active)

Use of Impersonal "it" In Passive Voice

We often use an impersonal "it" when we mention the words, thoughts or feelings of people in general.

PATTERN:

Active -- People **agree / assume / believe / decide / estimate / expect / feel / know / report / rumor / say / think / understand** (that) …
Passive -- It is **agreed / assumed / believed / decided / estimated / expected / felt / known / reported / rumored / said / thought / understood** that … (by people).

Active -- They **agreed / assumed / believed / decided / estimated / expected / felt / known / reported / rumored / said / thought / understood** (that) …
Passive -- It was **agreed / assumed / believed / decided / estimated / expected / felt / known / reported / rumored / said / thought / understood** that … (by them).

Active -- Everybody **agrees / assumes / believes / decides / estimates / expects / feels / knows / reports / rumors / says / thinks / understands** (that) …
Passive -- It is **agreed / assumed / believed / decided / estimated / expected / felt / known / reported / rumored / said / thought / understood** that … (by everybody).

Interchange of Active and Passive Voice

While changing active voice into passive voice, subject of active voice is moved into the position of object preceded by the preposition 'by' (optional), and object in active voice is moved into the position of subject. In other words, the places of subject and object in sentence are inter-changed in passive voice.

Also remember: Sometimes instead of using preposition 'by', you may have to use other prepositions.

Important Rules:
Changing Active Voice Into Passive Voice
Rule 1:
Check to see if the active sentence contains a direct object. If there is no direct object then the formation of passive voice is not possible.
If there is a direct object in the active sentence then the formation of passive voice is possible.
Move the **object** of the active voice into the position of **subject** (front of the sentence) in the passive voice. And move the **subject** of the active voice into the position of **object** in the passive voice.
Active -- They study grammar. [subject -- they; object -- grammar]
Passive -- Grammar **is studied** by them.

Note -- You can omit subject of active voice in passive voice if it gives enough meaning.
Active -- We should respect elders. [subject – we; direct object -- elders]
Passive -- Elders **should be respected** by us. Or
Passive -- Elders **should be respected**.

Rule 2:

Passive voice needs a **helping verb** to express the action. Put the helping verb in the same tense as the original active sentence. The **main verb** of the active voice is always changed into **past participle (third form of verb)** in different ways:

is / am / are / was / were + past participle

is / am / are / was / were + being + past participle

have been / has been / had been + past participle

will be / shall be / can be / may be + past participle

would be / could be / should be / might be + past participle

Very Important Note --

Auxiliary verbs in passive voice are used according to the tense of the sentence

The verb "to be" indicates the tense, and the past participle indicates the action.

Rule 3:

Place the active sentence's subject into a phrase beginning with the preposition **'by'**. In other words, the person or thing that makes the action is introduced by the preposition **'by'** in the passive.

Active -- I finished the work.

*Passive -- The work was finished **by** me.*

[Sometimes, others prepositions (at, in, with, for) are used instead of **by**]

Active -- He knows me.

*Passive -- I am known **to** him.*

Rule 4:

If the **subject** in an active voice sentence is a pronoun (I, we, you, he, she, they, it), it changes in passive voice sentence as follows:

"I" is changed into "me"

"We" is changed into "us"

"You" remains unchanged

"He" is changed into "him"

"She" is changed into "her"

"They" is changed into "them"

"It" remains unchanged

If the **object** in an active voice sentence is a pronoun (me, us, you, him, her, they, it), it changes in passive voice sentence as follows:

me -- I; us -- we; you -- you; him -- he; her -- she; them -- they; it -- it

Active -- **He** sent a message to **me**.
Passive -- **I** was sent a message by **him**.

Active -- **I** sent **him** a message.
Passive -- **He** was sent a message by **me**.

Rule 5:

Subject- Verb Agreement

Make the first verb agree with the new subject in passive voice.

Active -- **He threw** the balls. [subject of active voice -- He, verb -- threw]
Passive -- The **balls were** thrown by him. [subject of passive voice -- balls; first verb -- were]

Active -- **He threw** the ball. [subject of active voice -- He, verb -- threw]
Passive -- The **ball was** thrown by him. [subject of passive voice -- ball; first verb -- was]

Rule 6:

When there are two objects (direct object and indirect object), only one object is interchanged. The second object remains unchanged.

Active -- She gave me a laptop

[subject -- she; verb -- gave; indirect object -- me; direct object -- laptop]

Passive -- A **laptop** was given to **me** by her. Or

Passive -- I was given a **laptop** by her.

Difference between Direct and Indirect Object

Indirect Object is a noun, noun phrase or pronoun that refers to the person or thing that an action is done to or for.

Direct Object is a noun, noun phrase or pronoun that refers to a person or thing that is directly affected by the action of a verb

Examples:

Give *me newspaper*. [me = Indirect object; newspaper = direct object]

I bought *him a dictionary*. [him = indirect object; dictionary = direct object]

We helped *them* yesterday. [them =direct object].

SITUATIONS WHERE FORMATION OF PASSIVE VOICE IS NOT POSSIBLE:

(A). TENSES

Following Tenses Cannot Be Changed Into Passive Voice:

1. Present Perfect Continuous Tense

2. Past Perfect Continuous Tense

3. Future Continuous Tense

4. Future Perfect Continuous Tense

(B).TRANSITIVE AND INTRANISITIVE VERBS

Only the verb which takes direct object can go into the passive. **Intransitive verbs** can't be changed into passive voice because there is no object in intransitive verbs.

Note: There are two types of verbs

Transitive Verb -- Needs Object

Intransitive Verb -- Don't Need Object

Most verbs can be used both as transitive and as intransitive verbs. But there are many verbs which are used only intransitively.

Examples:

Active voice sentence with **transitive** verb - We **sent** a message.

There is a direct object - 'a message' - in this sentence. Thus, this sentence could be changed into passive voice:

Passive Voice -- A message was sent by us.

Active voice sentence with **intransitive** verb - We **sleep**.

There is no object in this sentence. (Thus, passive voice is not possible)

Verbs which are used only intransitively --

to become, to come, to denote, to die, to go, to fall, to happen, to occur, to rise, to sleep, to walk, etc.

STATIVE VERBS

Stative verbs are verbs which refer to states instead of actions. Stative verbs are generally not used in the passive voice.

Examples of stative verbs: contain, cost, see, hear, keep, lack, like, resemble, weigh, etc.

Active -- This computer **costs** one thousand dollars

INCORRECT -- This computer **is cost** one thousand dollars.

NO ONE AND NOBODY

Active -- **Nobody** understands him.
Passive -- He is **never** understood.

Active -- **Nobody** has understood me.
Passive -- I have **never** been understood.

Active -- **No one** ever said a word.
Passive -- A word was **never** said.

Common Patterns For Changing Active Voice Into Passive Voice Are As Follows:

1. First or Second Form of Verb

PRESENT INDEFINITE/SIMPLE TENSE

(I). AFFIRMATIVE SENTENCE

structure of active sentence --

subject + verb first form + object

structure of passive sentence --

object of the active sentence + am/is/are + past participle form of the verb + by + subject of the active sentence

Active -- He **gives** them reward.
Passive -- They **are given** reward by him.

Active – We **thump** the table.
Passive – The table **is thumped** by us.

(II). NEGATIVE SENTENCE

structure of active sentence --

subject + do/does + not + verb first form + object

structure of passive sentence --

object of the active sentence + am/is/are + not + past participle form of the verb + by + subject of the active sentence

Active – My students **do not call** me.
Passive – I **am not called** by my students.

Active -- John **does not teach** Paul.

Passive -- Paul **is not taught** by John.

Active – We **do not provoke** them.

Passive – They **are not provoked** by us.

(III). INTERROGATIVE SENTENCE

structure of active sentence --

do/does + subject + verb first form + object

structure of passive sentence --

am/is/are + object of the active sentence + past participle form of the verb + by + subject of the active sentence

Active -- **Does** she **watch** movie?

Passive -- **Is** movie **watched** by her?

NOTE:

When the active sentence begins with a question word, the passive sentence also begins with a question word.

Active -- **Why do** you **criticize** him?

Passive -- **Why was** he **criticized** by you?

PAST INDEFINITE/SIMPLE TENSE

(I). AFFIRMATIVE SENTENCE

structure of active sentence --

subject + verb second form + object

structure of passive sentence --

object of the active sentence + was/were + past participle form of the verb + by + subject of the active sentence

Active -- Joseph **helped** Morris.
Passive -- Morris **was helped** (by Joseph).

Active -- The audience loudly **cheered** the President's speech.
Passive -- The President's speech **was** loudly **cheered** (by the audience).

Active -- The Student Federation **awarded** him as the 'Best Scholar of the College'.
Passive -- He **was awarded** as the 'Best Scholar of the College' (by the Student Federation).

(II). NEGATIVE SENTENCE

structure of active sentence --

subject + did + not + verb first form + object

structure of passive sentence --

object of the active sentence + was/were + not + past participle form of the verb + by + subject of the active sentence

Active -- She **did not join** the party.
Passive -- The party **was not joined** (by her).

Active -- Monkeys **did not eat** the mangoes.
Passive -- Mangoes **were not eaten** (by monkeys).

(III). INTERROGATIVE SENTENCE

structure of active sentence --

did + subject + verb first form + object

structure of passive sentence --

was/were + object of the active sentence + past participle form of the verb + by + subject of the active sentence

Active -- **Did** scientists **develop** a new machine?
Passive -- **Was** a new machine **developed** (by scientists)?

Active -- **Did** the company **pay** salaries to the employees?
Passive -- **Were** the employees **paid** salaries (by the company)?

Active -- **Did** she **buy** golden necklace?
Passive -- **Was** golden necklace **bought** (by her)?

NOTE:

When the active sentence begins with a question word, the passive sentence also begins with a question word.

Active -- **How did** the lawyers **obtain** information?
Passive -- **How was** information **obtained** by the lawyers?

FUTURE INDEFINITE/SIMPLE TENSE

(I). AFFIRMATIVE SENTENCE

structure of active sentence --

subject + will/shall + verb first form + object

structure of passive sentence --

object of the active sentence + will/shall + be + past participle form of the verb + by + subject of the active sentence

Active -- People (They/Someone) **will admire** her.
Passive -- She **will be admired** (by people/them/someone).

(II). NEGATIVE SENTENCE

structure of active sentence --

subject + will/shall + not + verb first form + object

structure of passive sentence --

object of the active sentence + will/shall + not + be + past participle form of the verb + by + subject of the active sentence

Active -- Circumstances **will not oblige** me to go.
Passive -- I **shall not be obliged** to go (by circumstances).

(III). INTERROGATIVE SENTENCE

structure of active sentence --

will/shall + subject + verb first form + object

structure of passive sentence --

will/shall + object of the active sentence + be + past participle form of the verb + by + subject of the active sentence

Active -- **Will** teachers **make** him principal?

Passive -- **Will** he **be made** principal (by teachers)?

NOTE:

When the active sentence begins with a question word, the passive sentence also begins with a question word.

Active -- **When will** she book a ticket?

Passive -- **When will** a ticket **be booked** by her?

2. Auxiliary Verb 'Be' + -ING Form of Verb

(A). PRESENT CONTINUOUS TENSE

(I). AFFIRMATIVE SENTENCE

structure of active sentence --

subject + am/is/are + -ing form of verb + object

structure of passive sentence --

object of the active sentence + am/is/are + being + past participle form of the verb + by + subject of the active sentence

Active -- They **are watching** video.
Passive -- Video **is being watched** (by them).

Active -- A cat **is catching** mice.
Passive -- Mice **are being caught** (by a cat).

(II). NEGATIVE SENTENCE

structure of active sentence --

subject + am/is/are + not + -ing form of verb + object

structure of passive sentence --

object of the active sentence + am/is/are + not + being + past participle form of the verb + by + subject of the active sentence

Active -- He **is not chasing** me.
Passive -- I **am not being chased** (by him).

Active – The villagers **are not cutting** the grass.

Passive – The grass **is not being cut** (by the villagers).

(III). INTERROGATIVE SENTENCE

structure of active sentence --

am/is/are + subject + -ing form of verb + object

structure of passive sentence --

am/is/are + object of the active sentence + being + past participle form of the verb + by + subject of the active sentence

Active -- **Is** he **solving** this problem?

Passive -- **Is** this problem **being solved** (by him).

NOTE:

When the active sentence begins with a question word such as **how, when, which, whose, and why,** the passive sentence also begins with a question word.

Active -- **Why is** he **not accepting** my offer?

Passive -- **Why is** my offer **not being accepted** by him?

When the active sentence begins with '**whose**', the passive sentence begins with '**by whose**'.

Active -- **Whose** son **is troubling** you?

Passive -- **By whose** son **are you being troubled**?

When the active sentence begins with '**who**', the passive sentence begins with '**by whom**'.

Active -- **Who is** calling you?
Passive -- **By whom are you being** called?

When the active sentence begins with '**whom**', the passive sentence begins with '**who**'.
Active -- **Whom** are they **waiting** for?
Passive -- **Who are being waited for** by them?

PAST CONTINUOUS TENSE

(I). AFFIRMATIVE SENTENCE
structure of active sentence --

subject + was/were + -ing form of verb + object

structure of passive sentence --

object of the active sentence + was/were + being + past participle form of the verb + by + subject of the active sentence

Active -- Police personnel **were taking** him to prison.
Passive -- He **was being taken** to prison (by police personnel).

(II). NEGATIVE SENTENCE
structure of active sentence --

subject + was/were + not + -ing form of verb + object

structure of passive sentence --

object of the active sentence + was/were + not + being + past participle form of the verb + by + subject of the active sentence

Active -- We **were not playing** music.

Passive -- Music **was not being played** (by us).

(III). INTERROGATIVE SENTENCE

structure of active sentence --

was/were + subject + -ing form of verb + object

structure of passive sentence --

was/were + object of the active sentence + being + past participle form of the verb + by + subject of the active sentence

Active -- **Was** she **stealing** your money?

Passive -- **Was** your money **being stolen** (by her)?

NOTE:

When the active sentence begins with a question word, the passive sentence also begins with a question word.

Active -- **Why was** she **packing** a bag?

Passive -- **Why** a bag **was being packed** by her?

NOTE:

*Formation of Passive voice of **future continuous form** is not possible.*

3. Have/Has/Had + Past Participle

PRESENT PERFECT TENSE

(I). AFFIRMATIVE SENTENCE

structure of active sentence --

subject + have/has + past participle form of the verb + object

structure of passive sentence --

object of the active sentence + have/has + been + past participle form of the verb + by + subject of the active sentence

Active -- Children **have burst** the balloons.
Passive -- The balloons **have been burst** (by children).

Active -- Someone **has finished** my work.
Passive -- My work **has been finished** (by someone).

Active -- The manager **has appointed** ten sales girls.
Passive -- Ten sales girls **have been appointed** (by the manager).

Active -- One particular student **has answered** all the questions.
Passive -- All the questions **have been answered** (by one particular student).

(I). NEGATIVE SENTENCE

structure of active sentence --

subject + have/has + not + past participle form of the verb + object

structure of passive sentence --

object of the active sentence + have/has + not + been + past participle form of the verb + by + subject of the active sentence

Active -- They **have not identified** the mischief-makers.
Passive -- The mischief-makers **have not been identified** (by them).

Active -- The opponent **has not defeated** our team.
Passive -- Our team **has not been defeated** (by the opponent).

Active -- The department **has not delivered** the message.
Passive -- The message **has not been delivered** (by the department).

Active -- The Cabinet **has not postponed** the meeting.
Passive -- The meeting **has not been postponed** (by the Cabinet).

(III). INTERROGATIVE SENTENCE

structure of active sentence --

have/has + subject + past participle form of the verb + object

structure of passive sentence --

have/has + object of the active sentence + been + past participle form of the verb + by + subject of the active sentence

Active -- **Have** rescue workers **explained** the situation?
Passive -- **Has** the situation **been explained** (by rescue workers)?

Active -- **Have** they **received** payment?
Passive -- **Has** the payment **been received** (by them)?

Active -- **Has** he **finalized** the list of members?
Passive -- **Has** the list of members **been finalized** (by him)?

Active – **Has** she **run** a decorative items store?
Passive -- **Has** a decorative items store **been run** (by her?)

NOTE:

When the active sentence begins with a question word, the passive sentence also begins with a question word.

Active -- **How has** he **passed** the test?
Passive -- **How has** the test **been passed** by him?

PAST PERFECT TENSE

(I). AFFIRMATIVE SENTENCE

structure of active sentence --

subject + had + past participle form of the verb + object

structure of passive sentence --

object of the active sentence + had + been + past participle form of the verb + by + subject of the active sentence

Active -- She **had renewed** her passport.
Passive -- Her passport **had been renewed** (by her).

Active -- Gardener **had watered** the plants.
Passive -- The plants **had been watered** (by gardener).

Active -- They **had dispatched** helicopters with equipment and doctors to help extract and evacuate the survivors.

Passive -- Helicopters **had been dispatched** with equipment and doctors to help extract and evacuate the survivors.

(II). NEGATIVE SENTENCE

structure of active sentence --

subject + had + not + past participle form of the verb + object

structure of passive sentence --

object of the active sentence + had + not + been + past participle form of the verb + by + subject of the active sentence

Active -- His mother **had not rebuked** him.
Passive -- He **had not been rebuked** (by his mother).

Active -- She **had not paid** the house rent.
Passive -- The house rent **had not been paid** (by her).

(III). INTERROGATIVE SENTENCE

structure of active sentence --

had + subject + past participle form of the verb + object

structure of passive sentence --

had + object of the active sentence + been + past participle form of the verb + by + subject of the active sentence

Active -- **Had** the guard **closed** the main gate?

Passive -- **Had** the main gate **been closed** (by the guard)**?**

Active -- **Had** her father **saved** money for her education?
Passive -- **Had** money **been saved** for her education (by her father)?

NOTE:

When the active sentence begins with a question word, the passive sentence also begins with a question word.

Active -- **Where has** she **kept** the camera?
Passive -- **Where has** the camera **been kept** by her?

FUTURE PERFECT TENSE

(I). AFFIRMATIVE SENTENCE

structure of active sentence --

subject + will/shall + have + past participle form of the verb + object

structure of passive sentence --

object of the active sentence + will/shall + have + been + past participle form of the verb + by + subject of the active sentence

Active -- We **shall have recharged** our mobile phones.
Passive -- Our mobile phones **will have been recharged** (by us).

Active -- The judge **will have given** the verdict.
Passive -- The verdict **will have been given** (by the judge).

Active -- The forest officers **will have reopened** the Jim Corbett National Park for visitors.

Passive -- Jim Corbett National Park **will have been reopened** for visitors (by the forest officers).

(II). NEGATIVE SENTENCE

structure of active sentence --

subject + will/shall + not + have + past participle form of the verb + object

structure of passive sentence --

object of the active sentence + will/shall + not + have + been + past participle form of the verb + by + subject of the active sentence

Active -- We **will not have read** these novels.

Passive -- These novels **will not have been read** (by us).

(III). INTERROGATIVE SENTENCE

structure of active sentence --

will/shall + subject + have + past participle form of the verb + object

structure of passive sentence --

will/shall + object of the active sentence + have + been + past participle form of the verb + by + subject of the active sentence

Active -- **Will** she **have replaced** the book?

Passive – **Will** the book **have been replaced** (by her)?

Active -- **Will** he **have released** all birds?

Passive -- **Will** all birds **have been released** (by him)?

NOTE:

When the active sentence begins with a question word, the passive sentence also begins with a question word.

Active -- **When will** they **have placed** an order?

Passive -- **When will** an order **have been placed** by them?

4. Present/Future Modals + Verb Word

Present/Future Modals:

MAY, MIGHT, CAN, COULD, SHALL, SHOULD, WILL, WOULD, MUST, OUGHT TO

(I). AFFIRMATIVE SENTENCE

structure of active sentence --

subject + present/future modal verb + verb first form + object

structure of passive sentence --

object of the active sentence + present/future modal verb + be + past participle form of the verb + by + subject of the active sentence

Active -- I **may offer** him a job.

[There are two objects: indirect object -- 'him'; direct object -- 'a job')

Passive -- He **may be offered** a job (by me). Or

Passive -- A job **may be offered** to him (by me).

Active -- He **might learn** new language.

Passive -- New language **might be learnt** (by him).

Active -- I **can defeat** him.

Passive -- He **can be defeated** (by me).

Active -- You **could place** your bag over the table.

Passive -- Your bag **could be placed** over the table (by you).

Active -- We **shall invite** her in the function.

Passive -- She **will be invited** in the function (by us).

Active -- We **should promote** him immediately.

Passive -- He **should be promoted** immediately (by us).

Active -- The police **will investigate** the matter.

Passive -- The matter **will be investigated** (by the police).

Active -- She **would sing** a song.

Passive -- A song **would be sung** (by her).

Active -- They **must search** the missing kid.

Passive -- The missing kid **must be searched** (by them).

Active -- You **ought to follow** rules.

Passive -- Rules **ought to be followed** (by you).

(II). NEGATIVE SENTENCE

structure of active sentence --

subject + present/future modal verb + not + verb first form + object

structure of passive sentence --

object of the active sentence + present/future modal verb + not + be + past participle form of the verb + by + subject of the active sentence

Active -- I **may not offer** him a job.

[There are two objects: indirect object -- 'him'; direct object -- 'a job')

Passive -- He **may not be offered** a job (by me). Or

Passive -- A job **may not be offered** to him (by me).

Active -- He **might not learn** new language.
Passive -- New language **might not be learnt** (by him).

Active -- I **cannot defeat** him.
Passive -- He **cannot be defeated** (by me).

Active -- You **could not place** your bag over the table.
Passive -- Your bag **could not be placed** over the table (by you).

Active -- We **shall not invite** her in the function.
Passive -- She **will not be invited** in the function (by us).

Active -- We **should not promote** him immediately.
Passive -- He **should not be promoted** immediately (by us).

Active -- The police **will not investigate** the matter.
Passive -- The matter **will not be investigated** (by the police).

Active -- She **would not sing** a song.
Passive -- A song **would not be sung** (by her).

Active -- They **must not search** the missing kid.
Passive -- The missing kid **must not be searched** (by them).

Active -- You **ought not to follow** rules.
Passive -- Rules **ought not to be followed** (by you).

(I). INTERROGATIVE SENTENCE

structure of active sentence --

present/future modal verb + subject + verb first form + object

structure of passive sentence --

present/future modal verb + object of the active sentence + be + past participle form of the verb + by + subject of the active sentence

Active -- **May** I **open** the door?
Passive -- **May** the door **be opened** by me?

Active -- **Might he learn** new language?
Passive -- **Might** new language **be learnt** (by him)?

Active -- **Can** I **defeat** him?
Passive -- **Can** he **be defeated** (by me)?

Active -- **Could** you **place** your bag over the table?
Passive -- **Could** your bag **be placed** over the table (by you)?

Active -- **Shall** we **invite** her in the function?
Passive -- **Will** she **be invited** in the function (by us)?

Active -- **Should** we **promote** him immediately?
Passive -- **Should** he **be promoted** immediately (by us)?

Active -- **Will** the police **investigate** the matter?
Passive -- **Will** the matter **be investigated** (by the police)?

Active -- **Would** she **sing** a song?
Passive -- **Would** a song **be sung** (by her)?

Active -- **Must** they **search** the missing kid?

Passive -- **Must** the missing kid **be searched** (by them)?

Active -- **Ought** you **to follow** rules?

Passive -- **Ought** rules **to be followed** (by you)?

5. Past Modals + Past Participle

Past Modals:

May Have, Might Have, Could Have, Should Have, Would Have, Must Have

(I). AFFIRMATIVE SENTENCE

structure of active sentence --

subject + past modal verb + past participle form of the verb + object

structure of passive sentence --

object of the active sentence + past modal verb + been + past participle form of the verb + by + subject of the active sentence

Active -- He **may have heard** their conversation.
Passive -- Their conversation **may have been heard** (by him).

Active -- She **might have achieved** her target.
Passive -- Her target **might have been achieved** (by her).

Active -- You **could have won** the match.
Passive -- The match **could have been won** (by you).

Active -- You **should have called** his name.
Passive -- His name **should have been called** (by you).

Active -- She **would have sent** him money.
[There are two objects: 'him' and 'money')
Passive -- He **would have been sent** money (by her).
Passive -- Money **would have been sent** to him (by her).

Active -- She **must have studied** language rules.

Passive -- Language rules **must have been studied** (by her).

(I). NEGATIVE SENTENCE

structure of active sentence --

subject + negative form of past modal verb + past participle form of the verb + object

structure of passive sentence --

object of the active sentence + negative form of past modal verb + been + past participle form of the verb + by + subject of the active sentence

Negative Forms of "Past Modals" are as follows:

may have -- may not have

might have -- might not have

could have -- could not have

should have -- should not have

would have -- would not have

must have -- must not have

Active -- He **may not have heard** their conversation.

Passive -- Their conversation **may not have been heard** (by him).

Active -- She **might not have achieved** her target.

Passive -- Her target **might not have been achieved** (by her).

Active -- You **could not have won** the match.

Passive -- The match **could not have been won** (by you).

Active -- You **should not have called** his name.

Passive -- His name **should not have been called** (by you).

Active -- She **would not have sent** him money.

[There are two objects: indirect object -- 'him'; direct object -- 'money')

Passive -- He **would not have been sent** money (by her).

Passive -- Money **would not have been sent** to him (by her).

Active -- She **must not have studied** language rules.

Passive -- Language rules **must not have been studied** (by her).

6. Verb ± Preposition

structure of passive sentence --

object of the active sentence + auxiliary verb + past participle form of the verb + preposition + by + subject of the active sentence

When the verb is followed by a preposition-

Active -- The kids **laughed at** the clown.

In this sentence, noun '**clown**' is the object of the preposition **at**, and not the verb 'laughed'. This sentence can be changed into the passive as follows:

Passive -- The clown **was laughed at** by the kids.

Other Examples:

Active -- I **look after** him.

Passive -- He **is looked after** (by me).

In continuous tense, use '**being**' after auxiliary verb in passive voice

Active -- I **am searching for** him.

Passive -- He **is being searched for** (by me).

Note: If there is modal verb in active voice than use "**modal verb + be + past participle**" in passive voice.

Active -- He **will look after** you well.

Passive -- You **will be well-looked after** (by him).

7. Main Verb + Object + Complement

structure of passive sentence --

object of the active sentence + auxiliary verb + past participle form of the verb + complement + by + subject of the active sentence

Active -- They **called** the building magnificent.
Passive -- The building **was called** magnificent (by them).

Active -- We **consider** her well-mannered.
Passive -- She **is considered** well-mannered (by us).

Active -- Students **will choose** her monitor.
Passive -- She **will be chosen** monitor (by students).

Active -- Public **made** him leader.
Passive -- He **was made** leader (by public).

8. Main Verb + Object + Object

Some verbs can have two objects --

an **indirect object** (the person receiving something)

a **direct object** (the thing that someone gives)

If there are two objects in active voice then there could be two passive voice sentences. Either

object can become the subject of the verb in the passive Voice. The object which does not become the

subject remains as an object.

We can use the following two patterns in active voice --

(i). verb + indirect object + direct object

(ii). verb + direct object + to + indirect object

"to + indirect object" pattern is used with the following verbs:

allow, bring, convey, give, grant, hand, lend, lob, offer, owe, pass, pay,

promise, provide, read, sell, send, show, supply, take, teach, tell, throw, write,

etc.

Active -- He **gives** *me a book.* Or- He **gives** *a book to me.*

[Two objects: indirect object -- me, direct object -- a book]

We can use the following two patterns in passive voice --

(i). **indirect object of the active sentence + be + past participle form of the verb + direct object + by + subject of the active sentence**

Passive -- I **am given** a book (by him).

(ii). **direct object of the active sentence + be + past participle form of the verb + to + indirect object + by + subject of the active sentence**

Passive -- A book **is given** to me (by him).

Additional Examples --

Active -- She **owed** *her friend hundred dollars.* Or- She **owed** *hundred dollars to her friend.*

[Two objects: indirect object -- her, direct object -- money]

Passive -- Her friend was **owed** hundred dollars (by her). **OR**

Passive -- Hundred dollars were **owed** to her friend (by her).

Active -- He **gifted** *me a Smartphone.* Or- He **gifted** *a Smartphone to me.*

[Two objects: indirect object -- me, direct object -- a Smartphone]

Passive -- I **was gifted** a Smartphone (by him). **OR**

Passive -- A Smartphone **was gifted** to me (by him).

Active -- We **will send** *him an invitation.* Or- We **will send** *an invitation to him.*

[Two objects: indirect object -- him, direct object -- invitation]

Passive -- He **will be sent** an invitation (by us). **OR**

Passive -- An invitation **will be sent** to him (by us).

Active -- President **offered** *her a ministerial post.* Or- President **offered** *a ministerial post to her.*

[Two objects: indirect object -- her, direct object -- a ministerial post]

Passive -- She **was offered** a ministerial post (by President). **OR**

Passive -- A ministerial post **was offered** to her (by President).

Active -- Mr. Stephen **taught** *me web-designing.* Or- Mr. Stephen **taught** *web-designing to me.*

[Two objects: indirect object -- us, direct object -- web designing]

Passive -- I **was taught** *web-designing* (by Mr. Stephen). **OR**

Passive -- Web-designing **was taught** to me (by Mr. Stephen).

Active -- The teacher **will give** *you an assignment.* Or- The teacher **will give** *an assignment to you.*

[Two objects: indirect object -- you, direct object -- an assignment]

Passive -- You **will be given** an assignment (by the teacher). **OR**

Passive -- An assignment **will be given** to you (by the teacher).

Important Note:

We can also use 'for + indirect object' instead of 'to + indirect object' in active voice

"for + Indirect object" pattern is used with the following verbs:

book, bring, build, buy, choose, cook, fetch, find, get, leave, make, obtain, order, pick, reserve, save, select, etc.

With these verbs, we make passive voice only by placing direct object of active voice sentence in the position of subject in passive construction. We generally avoid placing indirect object of active voice sentence in the position of subject in passive construction.

Active -- He **fetched** *me some food.* Or- He **fetched** *some food for me.*

[Two objects: indirect object -- me, direct object -- some food]

Passive -- Some food was fetched for me (by him).

You should avoid the following pattern --

Passive -- I was fetched some food (by him).

9. Have/Has/Had + Infinitive (To + Verb)

Note -- 'Have To / Has To / Had To' Imply Compulsion/Obligation/Necessity, Etc.

(I). AFFIRMATIVE SENTENCE

structure of active sentence --

subject + have/has/had + to + verb + object

structure of passive sentence --

object of the active sentence + have/has/had + to + be + past participle form of the verb + by + subject of the active sentence

Active -- You **have to finish** dinner.
Passive -- Dinner **has to be finished** (by you).

Active -- He **has to return** my money.
Passive -- My money **has to be returned** (by him).

Active -- The officer **had to report** the matter.
Passive -- The matter **had to be reported** (by the officer).

(II). NEGATIVE SENTENCE

structure of active sentence --

subject + have/has/had + not + to + verb + object

structure of passive sentence --

object of the active sentence + have/has/had + not + to + be + past participle form of the verb + by + subject of the active sentence

Active -- They **have not to face** opposition.

Passive -- Opposition **has not to be faced** (by them).

Active -- She **has not to open** a saving account.

Passive -- Saving account **has not to be opened** (by her).

Active -- They **had not to attend** the meeting.

Passive -- The meeting **had not to be attended** (by them).

(I). INTERROGATIVE SENTENCE

structure of active sentence --

have/has/had + subject + to + verb + object

structure of passive sentence --

have/has/had + object of the active sentence + to + be + past participle form of the verb + by + subject of the active sentence

Active -- **Have** they **to finish** the work?

Passive -- **Has** the work **to be finished** (by them)?

Active -- **Has** he **to make** special arrangements for the seniors?

Passive -- **Has** special arrangements **to be made** for the seniors (by him)?

Active -- **Had** we **to assist** him?

Passive -- **Had** he **to be assisted** (by us)?

10. Auxiliary Verb 'Be' + Infinitive (To + Verb)

(I). AFFIRMATIVE SENTENCE

structure of active sentence --

subject + am/is/are/was/were + infinitive (to + verb) + object

structure of passive sentence --

object of the active sentence + am/is/are/was/were + to + be + past participle form of the verb + by + subject of the active sentence

Active -- She **is to take** the baby away.
Passive -- The baby **is to be taken** away (by her)**.**

Active -- The Prime Minister **is to address** the nation.
Passive -- The nation **is to be addressed** (by the Prime Minister).

Active -- They **were to bring** doctor.
Passive -- Doctor **was to be brought** (by them).

(I). NEGATIVE SENTENCE

structure of active sentence --

subject + am/is/are/was/were + not + infinitive (to + verb) + object

structure of passive sentence --

object of the active sentence + am/is/are/was/were + not + to + be + past participle form of the verb + by + subject of the active sentence

Active -- We **are not to attend** the conference.
Passive -- The conference **is not to be attended** (by us).

Manik Joshi

Active -- She **was not to make** a phone call.

Passive -- Phone call **was not to be made** (by her).

(I). INTERROGATIVE SENTENCE

structure of active sentence --

am/is/are/was/were + subject + infinitive (to + verb) + object

structure of passive sentence --

am/is/are/was/were + object of the active sentence + to + be + past participle form of the verb + by + subject of the active sentence

Active -- **Is** he **to finish** the homework?

Passive -- **Is** the homework **to be finished** (by him)**?**

Active -- **Am** I **to help** him?

Passive -- **Is** he **to be helped** (by me)?

11. <u>Verb</u> + <u>Object</u> + <u>Infinitive</u> (Without 'To')

structure of active sentence --

subject + verb + object + infinitive (without 'to)

structure of passive sentence --

object of the active sentence + auxiliary verb + past participle form of the verb + to + infinitive (without 'to') + by + subject of the active sentence

Active -- My mother **saw** me **play** a game.

Passive -- I **was seen to play** a game (by my mother).

[In active voice, there is infinitive (without 'to') -- **play**

In passive voice, we have added '**to'** before **play**]

Active -- Gardener **caught** him **pluck** the flower.

Passive -- He **was caught to pluck** the flower (by gardener).

[In active voice, there is infinitive (without 'to') -- **pluck**

In passive voice, we have added '**to'** before **pluck**]

Active -- I **found** him **tease** the kid.

Passive -- He **was found to tease** the kid (by me).

[In active voice, there is infinitive (without 'to') -- **tease**

In passive voice, we have added '**to'** before **tease**]

Active -- I **made** him **stand** up.

Passive -- He **was made to stand** up (by me).

[In active voice, there is infinitive (without 'to') -- **stand**

In passive voice, we have added '**to'** before **stand**]

MORE EXAMPLES:

Active -- Teacher **made** him **study**.

Passive -- He **was made to study** (by teacher).

Active -- I **saw** him **go**.

Passive -- He **was seen to go** (by me).

Active -- The President **will make** the minister **resign** from his post.

Passive -- The minister **will be made to resign** from his post (by the President).

12. There ± Verb 'Be' ± Noun ± Infinitive

structure of active sentence --
There + verb 'be' + noun + infinitive ('to + verb')

structure of passive sentence --
There + verb 'be' + noun + to + be + past participle form of the verb

Active -- There is an assignment **to finish**.
Passive -- There is an assignment **to be finished**.

Active -- There is no time **to lose**.
Passive -- There is no time **to be lost**.

Active -- There is no money **to waste**.
Passive -- There is no money **to be wasted**.

Active -- There was no item **to consume**.
Passive -- There was no item **to be consumed**.

Active -- There was an issue **to resolve**.
Passive -- There was an issue **to be resolved**.

Active -- There are so many books **to read**.
Passive -- There are so many books **to be read**.

Active -- There were many spots **to travel**.
Passive -- There were many spots **to be travelled**.

Also Note: It Is + To + Verb

[Use "To + Be + Past Participle" In Passive Voice]

Active -- It is time **to shut** up the office.

Passive -- It is time **for** the office **to be shut up**.

Active -- It is great **to help** the poor people.

Passive -- It is great **for** the poor people **to be helped**.

Active -- It is time **to switch off** the TV.

Passive -- It is time **for** the TV **to be switched off**.

13. Interrogative Sentences

(i) Interrogative Sentences Using Auxiliary Verb

Active -- **Did** she **scold** you?
Passive -- **Were** you **scolded** (by her)?

Active -- **Will** he **develop** a website?
Passive -- **Will** a website **be developed** (by him)?

Active -- **Has** she **written** a script?
Passive -- **Has** a script **been written** (by her)?

Active -- **Had** they **helped** the boy?
Passive -- **Had** the boy **been helped** (by them)?

(ii) Interrogative Sentences Using 'Who'

Active -- Who **present** you this book?
Passive -- By whom **was** this book **presented** to you? **OR**
Passive -- By whom **were** you **presented** this book? **OR**
Passive -- Who **was** this book **presented** to you by?

Active -- Who can **keep** this money?
Passive -- By whom can this money **be kept**? **OR**
Passive -- Who can this money **be kept** by?

Active -- Who **gave** you box?
Passive -- By whom **was** box **given** to you? **OR**

Passive -- By whom **were** you **given** box? **OR**

Passive -- Who **was** box **given** to you by?

(iii) Interrogative Sentences: Indirect Question

Active -- He **asked** Martina if she was ill.

Passive -- Martina **was asked** if she was ill.

Active -- I **asked** her when she would revisit.

Passive -- She **was asked** when she would revisit.

Active -- I **asked** him if he is reading a novel.

Passive -- He **was asked** if he was reading a novel.

Active -- They **ask** me if I am watching movie.

Passive -- I **am asked** if I am watching movie.

14. Imperative Sentences

Imperative sentences are used to give commands/suggestion/instruction/warning/advice.

In imperative sentence, subject - 'you' - is understood

structure of active sentence --

verb + object

structure of passive sentence --

let + object of the active sentence + be + past participle form of the verb

OR

object of the active sentence + should + be + past participle

(i) Imperative Sentences: Order/Command

Active -- **Bring** a golden ring.
Passive -- **Let** a golden ring **be brought**.

Active -- **Turn** her out.
Passive -- **Let** her **be turned** out.

Active -- **Pass** the order.
Passive -- **Let** the order **be passed**.

Active -- **Rebuke** him.
Passive -- **Let** him **be rebuked**.

Active -- **Ask** him to get up

Manik Joshi

Passive -- **Let** him **be asked** to get up.

(ii) Imperative Sentences: Advice

Active -- **Love** the earth.

Passive -- **Let** the earth **be loved. OR**

Passive -- The earth **should be loved**.

Active -- **Finish** your homework.

Passive -- **Let** your homework **be finished. OR**

Passive -- Your homework **should be finished**.

Active -- **Feed** the baby.

Passive -- **Let** the baby **be fed. OR**

Passive -- The baby **should be fed**.

Active -- **Help** your colleagues.

Passive -- **Let** your colleagues **be helped. OR**

Passive -- Your colleagues **should be helped**.

Active -- **Keep** your promise.

Passive -- Promise **should be kept**.

Active -- Don't **promote** unruliness.

Passive -- Unruliness **shouldn't be promoted**.

Also note the following examples for changing imperative sentences from active to passive voice:

Active -- **Be off** my sight.

Passive -- You **are <u>requested</u> to be off** my sight.

Active -- Don't **smoke**.

Passive -- You **are <u>ordered</u> not to smoke.**

<u>ALSO</u> <u>NOTE</u>--
<u>Indirect</u> <u>Command/Request</u>

Active -- I **told** him to make coffee.

Passive -- He **was told** to make coffee.

Active -- He **requested** her to lend him her book.

Passive -- She **was requested** to lend him her book.

15. Principal Clause + That + Noun Clause (Object)

(1). We can begin the passive form of these sentences with the subject of that-clause.

(2). We can begin the passive form of these sentences with "It is..."

Active -- People **consider** that he is wise. [= people consider him to be wise.]
Passive -- He **is considered** to be wise. **OR**
Passive -- It **is considered** that he is wise.

Active -- We **know** that some people are super achiever.
Passive -- Some people **are known** to be super achiever. **OR**
Passive -- It **is known** that some people are super achiever.

Active -- Many **think** that we are intelligent.
Passive -- We **are thought** to be intelligent. **OR**
Passive -- It **is thought** that we are intelligent.

Also Note:
Principal Clause + That + Subject + Should be + Past Participle [Passive Voice]
[You may remove 'that + subject', and replace 'should be + past participle' with "to be + past participle"]

Passive -- He wants that he **should be treated** as a minister.
Passive -- He wants **to be treated** as a minister.

Passive -- He likes that he **should be rewarded**.

Passive -- He likes **to be rewarded**.

Passive -- Employees think that they **should be promoted**.

Passive -- Employees think **to be promoted**.

16. Verb followed by --ING form or an Infinitive

Following verbs can be followed by either an **--ing form** or an **infinitive** -- **allow**, **advise**, **permit** and **forbid**.

PATTERN -- 1 -- WITH TO-INFINITIVE

structure of active sentence --

subject + verb + object + to-infinitive + phrase

Active -- We advise students **to prepare** for the exams.

structure of passive sentence --

object of the active sentence + auxiliary verb + past participle form of the verb + to-infinitive + phrase

Passive -- Students are advised **to prepare** for the exams.

PATTERN -- 2 -- WITH -ING FORM OF VERB

structure of active sentence --

subject + verb + -ing form of verb (object) + phrase

Active -- The government has forbidden **smoking** in public places.

structure of passive sentence --

object of the active sentence + auxiliary verb + past participle form of the verb + phrase

Passive -- Smoking has been forbidden in public places

17. Use of Prepositions

Preposition 'by' is commonly used in passive voice. But sometimes you are supposed to use other preposition instead of 'by'. Following are some examples:

Active -- He **satisfied** everybody.
Passive -- Everybody **was satisfied** *with* him.

Active -- He **knows** me.
Passive -- I **am known** *to* him.

Active -- Her conduct **shocked** me.
Passive -- I **was shocked** *at* her conduct.

Active -- This place **has** greatly **interested** me.
Passive -- I **have been** greatly **interested** *in* this place.

Active -- His manners **vex** me sometimes.
Passive -- I **am** sometimes **vexed** *at* his manners.

Note: in the following sentence, 'knife' is not agent/doer.
Passive -- The vegetable **can be cut** *with* a knife (by people).
You cannot make active of this sentence as follows:
INCORRECT -- A knife can cut the vegetable.
You should make active of this sentence as follows:
CORRECT -- People **can cut** the vegetable with a knife.

18. The Passive With Get

We sometimes uses **get** in the passive instead of **be**. We use **get + past participle** for something happening by accident, or in an unexpected or unplanned way. We use **get** in passive to emphasise action or change.

Many people **get injured** or **killed** in road accidents every day. = Many people **are injured** or **killed** in road accidents every day.
River **got swollen** due to heavy rains. = River **was swollen** due to heavy rains.
Her money **had got stolen**. = Her money **had been stolen**.

useful idiomatic expressions with **get** in passive voice:
get affected / get cancelled / get caught / get crushed / get delayed / get disconnected / get done / get duped / get filled / get formed / get impacted / get involved / get married / get paid / get started / get stuck / get transformed / get united / get wasted

19. Middle Voice

An **ergative verb** can change an object into a subject without needing to use a passive. This is sometimes called the 'middle voice'.

An **ergative verb** can be used in both a transitive and an intransitive way with the same meaning, where the object of the transitive verb is the same as the subject of the intransitive verb.

Active -- He **dropped** the pen.
In this sentence, there is emphasis on actor/doer (he).

Passive -- The pen **was dropped** by him
In this sentence, there is emphasis on object (pen) of the active voice.

Middle -- The pen **dropped**. [dropped = ergative verb]
In this sentence, there is emphasis on action ('dropped').

Active -- The health department **began** a new project.
In this sentence, there is emphasis on actor/doer (health department).

Passive -- A new project **was begun** by the health department.
In this sentence, there is emphasis on object (project) of the active voice.

Middle -- A new project **began**. [began = ergative verb]
In this sentence, there is emphasis on action ('began').

Exercise -- 01

Turn the following from Active Voice to Passive Voice or from Passive Voice to Active Voice

01. *Active* -- All the students passed the English test.

01. *Passive* -- ....

02. *Active* -- The storm uprooted the trees.

02. *Passive* -- ....

03. *Active* -- The driver slammed on the brakes as the bus sped downhill.

03. *Passive* -- ....

04. *Active* -- Climate change has intensified summer droughts and winter colds.

04. *Passive* -- ....

05. *Active* -- They have joined my team without terms and conditions.

05. *Passive* -- ....

06. *Active* -- Stinging cold in the air forced residents to remain indoors.

06. *Passive* -- ....

07. *Active* -- Villagers have been grappling with absence of a road for almost a decade.

07. *Passive* -- ....

08. *Active* -- Twist the wire.

08. *Passive --* ....

09. *Passive --* The project has to be finished by her.
09. *Active --* ....

10. *Passive --* The streets and houses of the city were flooded with water.
10. *Active --* ....

11. *Passive --* Enough development have been led by them in the society.
11. *Active --* ....

12. *Passive --* Many schemes are being formulated by the government for checking migration and development of remote areas.
12. *Active --*

....
....

13. *Passive --* The police teams were asked to maintain vigil on all vehicles and check passengers travelling by public transport.
13. *Active --*

....
....

14. *Passive --* It is expected by authorities that the rules will be followed by the citizens.
14. *Active --* ....

15. *Passive --* Was the beggar looked after by you?
15. *Active --* ....

Answers to the Exercise -- 01 --

01. *Passive* -- The English test **was passed** by all the students

02. *Passive* -- The trees **were uprooted** by the storm.

03. *Passive* -- The brakes **were slammed on** by the driver as the bus sped downhill.

04. *Passive* -- Summer droughts and winter colds **have been intensified** by climate change.

05. *Passive* -- My team **has been joined** by them without terms and conditions.

06. *Passive* -- Residents **were forced** to remain indoors by stinging cold in the air.

07. *Passive* -- "perfect continuous tense doesn't have passive voice".

08. *Passive* -- Let the wire **be twisted**

09. *Active* -- She **has to finish** the project

10. *Active* -- Water **flooded** the streets and houses of the city.

11. *Active* -- They **have led** enough development in the society.

12. *Active* -- The government **is formulating** many schemes for checking migration and development of remote areas.

13. *Active* -- They **asked** the police teams to maintain vigil on all vehicles and check passengers travelling by public transport.

14. *Active* -- Authorities expect that the rules will be followed by the citizens. Or Authorities expect the citizens to follow the rules.

15. *Active* -- Did you look after the beggar?

Exercise -- 02

Multiple-choice Test:-

01. *Active* -- She has to finish the project
01. *Passive* -- The project .... by her
(a). have to be finished
(b). had to finished
(c). has to be finished
(d). has revolved

02. *Active* -- They will take up counting of votes together in all the states.
02. *Passive* -- Counting of votes .... together in all the states.
(a). will have been taking up
(b). will be taken up
(c). will have been taken up
(d). will have taken up

03. *Active* -- I have laid down certain rules for him.
03. *Passive* -- Certain rules .... for him.
(a). were driven
(b). was being driven
(c). was driven
(d). have been laid down

04. *Active* -- He could not give any media interviews.
04. *Passive* -- Any media interviews .... by him.
(a). could not have been given

b). could not to have given

c). could not be given

d). could not have given

05. *Active* -- An old man was driving the car.

05. *Passive* -- The car .... by an old man.

(a). were driven

(b). was being driven

(c). was driven

(d). were been driven

06. *Active* -- They started a campaign to spread awareness on the
importance on education.

06. *Passive* -- A campaign .... to spread
awareness on the importance on education (by them).

(a). was started

(b). had started

(c). had been started

(d). is started

07. *Active* -- The teacher told him not to talk in class.

07. *Passive* -- He .... in class by the teacher.

(a). is told to not talk

(b). had been told not to talk

(c). was told not to talk

(d). told was not to talked

08. *Active* -- You should have made all efforts to avoid controversies.

08. *Passive* -- All efforts .... to avoid
controversies.

(a). should have had made

(b). should have been made

(c). should have to be made

(d). should had had made

09. *Active* -- Are you rethinking your decision?

09. Passive -- Is your decision .... by you?

(a). being rethought

(b). was rethought

(c). been rethought

(d). being to rethought

10. *Active* -- Why does everyone blame me?

10. Passive – Why .... by everyone.

(a). I was blamed

(b). do I blamed

(c). I had blamed

(d). am I blamed

Answers to the Exercise -- 02 --

01. (c). has to be finished | 02. (b). will be taken up | 03. (d). have been laid down | 04 (c). could not be given | 05. (b). was being driven | 06. (a). was started | 07. (c). was told not to talk | 08. (b). should have been made | 09. (a.) being rethought | 10. (d). am I blamed

Exercise -- 03

Determine whether each of the following statements is true or false.

01. We often use an impersonal "it" when we mention the words, thoughts or feelings of people in general.

(a). true | (b). false

02. We should never use **get** in the passive instead of **be**.

(a). true | (b). false

03. An intransitive verb can be used in the passive voice.

(a). true | (b). false

04. The passive voice is preferred when the actor is either unknown or unimportant.

(a). true | (b). false

05. If there is no direct object then formation of passive voice is not possible.

(a). true | (b). false

06. The active voice is preferred over the passive voice.

(a). true | (b). false

07. The active is often used in news reports.

(a). true | (b). false

08. When the active sentence begins with a question word such as how, when, which, whose, and why, the passive sentence also begins with a question word.

(a). **true** | (b). **false**

09. Future continuous tense and future perfect continuous tense can be changed from active voice into passive voice.
(a). **true** | (b). **false**

10. An **ergative verb** can be used in both a transitive and an intransitive way with the same meaning (a). **true** | (b). **false**

Answers to the Exercise -- 03 --
01. **true** | 02. **false** | 03. **false** | 04. **true** | 05. **true** | 06. **true** | 07. **false** | 08. **true** | 09. **false** | 10. **true**

****

About the Author

Manik Joshi, the author of this book was born on **Jan 26, 1979** at Ranikhet and is permanent resident of Haldwani, Kumaon zone of India. He is an Internet Marketer by profession. He is interested in domaining (business of buying and selling domain names), web designing (creating websites), and various online jobs (including 'self-publishing'). He is science graduate with ZBC (zoology, botany, and chemistry) subjects. He is also an MBA (with specialization in marketing). He has done three diploma courses in computer too. **ManikJoshi.com** is the personal website of the author.

Amazon Author Page of Manik Joshi:

https://www.amazon.com/author/manikjoshi

Email:

mail@manikjoshi.com

****

BIBLIOGRAPHY

'ENGLISH DAILY USE' TITLES BY MANIK JOSHI

01. How to Start a Sentence
02. English Interrogative Sentences
03. English Imperative Sentences
04. Negative Forms in English
05. Learn English Exclamations
06. English Causative Sentences
07. English Conditional Sentences
08. Creating Long Sentences in English
09. How to Use Numbers in Conversation
10. Making Comparisons in English
11. Examples of English Correlatives
12. Interchange of Active and Passive Voice
13. Repetition of Words
14. Remarks in English Language
15. Using Tenses in English
16. English Grammar- Am, Is, Are, Was, Were
17. English Grammar- Do, Does, Did
18. English Grammar- Have, Has, Had
19. English Grammar- Be and Have
20. English Modal Auxiliary Verbs
21. Direct and Indirect Speech
22. Get- Popular English Verb
23. Ending Sentences with Prepositions
24. Popular Sentences in English
25. Common English Sentences
26. Daily Use English Sentences
27. Speak English Sentences Everyday
28. Popular English Idioms and Phrases
29. Common English Phrases
30. Daily English- Important Notes

ENGLISH WORD POWER' TITLES BY MANIK JOSHI

01. Dictionary of English Synonyms
02. Dictionary of English Antonyms
03. Homonyms, Homophones and Homographs
04. Dictionary of English Capitonyms
05. Dictionary of Prefixes and Suffixes
06. Dictionary of Combining Forms
07. Dictionary of Literary Words
08. Dictionary of Old-fashioned Words
09. Dictionary of Humorous Words
10. Compound Words in English
11. Dictionary of Informal Words
12. Dictionary of Category Words
13. Dictionary of One-word Substitution
14. Hypernyms and Hyponyms
15. Holonyms and Meronyms
16. Oronym Words in English
17. Dictionary of Root Words
18. Dictionary of English Idioms
19. Dictionary of Phrasal Verbs
20. Dictionary of Difficult Words

OTHER TITLES BY MANIK

01. English Word Exercises (Part 1)
02. English Word Exercises (Part 2)
03. English Word Exercises (Part 3)
04. English Sentence Exercises
05. Test Your English
06. Match the Two Parts of the Words
07. Letter-Order In Words
08. Simple, Compound, Complex, & Compound-Complex Sentences
09. Transitional Words and Phrases
10. Regular and Irregular Verbs

****

Made in the USA
San Bernardino, CA
01 July 2017